The Art of Dying

From mountain pass to storm-tossed seashore, from
Barcelona to the Drakensberg, these new poems by
Adam Wyeth feature journeys both witty and
surreal. There is much that is busy transforming
here, from kitchen to ice-rink; rock to hatching egg.
In the richly imagined Talking Tree Alphabet, a birch
tree becomes Marilyn Monroe holding down her
skirt, while the blackthorn is a 'ravaged whore'. At
the heart of the collection, the still point around
which the energies flow, is a boy's relationship with
his father, the absurd indignity of death, and the
ceaseless unfolding of the generations: 'An ancient
vellum/ where the next life is written'. Language,
the raw material of the poet who shapes and makes
sense of the world, is celebrated without forgetting
the humble source of it all, Yeats's foul rag and bone
shop, or 'thorns/that draw blood and score the heart
completely' (from 'Gorse'). Dancing on the edge of
civilization, preferring the energizing potential of
dream and myth, Wyeth's is a refreshing new voice
on the Irish poetry scene.

KATIE DONOVAN

The Art of Dying

ADAM WYETH

In Memory

salmonpoetry

*Celebrating 35 Years
of Literary Publishing*

Published in 2016 by
Salmon Poetry
Cliffs of Moher, County Clare, Ireland
Website: www.salmonpoetry.com
Email: info@salmonpoetry.com

ISBN 978-1-910669-59-4

COVER IMAGE: *Fly dear © Nuvolanevicata | Dreamstime.com*
COVER DESIGN & BOOK TYPESETTING: *Siobhán Hutson*
Printed in Ireland by Sprint Print

Salmon Poetry gratefully acknowledges the support of
The Arts Council / An Chomhairle Ealaoín

for Kalai, Tadhg & Nathan

'This one is for the children.'
from *Idioteque*, Radiohead

Acknowledgements

Some of these poems have previously appeared in the following publications and programmes:

'Metamorphosis' and 'Oak' were published in *Poetry Ireland Review: Rising Generation* edition 2016; 'Girl with a Bag in Barcelona' was a runner-up in the Ballymaloe International Poetry Competition 2012 and published in *the Moth*; 'The World' was published in the *Irish Times*, 2016; 'Anatadaiphobia' was shortlisted in the Bridport International Poetry Competition and published in *Even the Daybreak: 35 Years of Salmon Poetry* (Salmon, 2016) and read on RTE Radio 1, *Arena*, 2016; 'Periwinkling' and 'Angry Birds' were published in the *Café Review*, Special Irish Edition; a version of 'Road Signs' was published in the *Stony Thursday Book*; 'Aisling' was published in the *Cork Literary Review*; 'Visiting the Poet' was published in the *Stony Thursday Book* special edition; 'The Flesh and the Spirit' was published in *Prelude* (US), 'Apollinaire Smoking' and 'Willow' were published in *Southword*; 'Rag and Bone Man' was published in *Dear World, An Anthology of Poems on Environmental Themes* (UK), 'The Great Book of Ireland' was commissioned by University College Cork and published in the anthology *New Eyes on the Great Book*, 2014. A version of 'Pine' was published under a different title in *A Riddle Fence Special Edition of Irish Poetry* in exchange with *Southword*; 'Chestnut' was published in *Cyphers*, 2016.

My heartfelt thanks go to Nuala Ní Chonchúir, Harry Clifton, Katie Donovan, Elaine Feeney, Leontia Flynn, Dave Lordan, Michael O'Loughlin, Mary O'Malley, Afric McGlinchey, Paula McGlinchey, Susan McKeown, Belinda McKeon, Alan McMonagle, Maeve O'Sullivan, Mary Noonan and Vincent Woods.

Contents

'Everything that lives must pass through many deaths.'

Carl Jung

Metamorphosis

The words are turning in on themselves
and then turning into something else.
They are turning over and under like birds
dipping in water, turning the reflection
of trees into rings and ripples in the lake.
They are asleep and then they wake
in the whiteness of the page. Black-licked
words fall like leaves littering the reflection
of the day, then are released birds.

Girl with a Bag in Barcelona

What was in the bag of the girl who had
just arrived in Barcelona? She sat down
on a bench and unfolded a piece of paper
that contained the address of her final destination.

At the moment of her taking out a cigarette
and assisting a passer-by with a light,
another man leaned over and placed his hand
on her bag, taking it away so simply,

I assumed he was a friend playing a joke,
until he broke into a bolt and the passer-by
turned cold as he ran after his accomplice,
flicking the cigarette over his shoulder

that sparked a trail before going out.
By the time I'd shot up and shouted, *Thieves!* —
they were halfway across Plaça de Catalunya
disappearing among the throng on La Rambla.

The girl didn't move and went on smoking
like nothing had happened, as if she didn't care,
taking long draws on her cigarette.
Perhaps there was nothing of value in the bag:

a magazine, toothbrush, tampons, dirty underwear.
On the other hand, perhaps her stillness was a sign
that there were items of overwhelming cost:
legal documents, her great grandmother's watch,

a diamond ring, a signed copy of *Ulysses*, first edition.
'Should I call the police?' I asked, sitting back down.
She gave a shrug that showed the futility of my question.
She seemed to have complete self-control,

I thought she might be a pupil of the mysterious
Tibetan school who acquire material possessions
only so they can let them go: to learn the art
of dying, slipping away quietly between

thoughts when no one is looking. The thieves
by now had been swallowed into the underbelly
of Barri Gòtic; prising open their booty
like ravens scrapping over road kill.

The bag, the cigarette, the moment,
snatched like a loose thought tossed to one side.
While high above the muggy streets, behind
the velvet-curtained sky, a satellite spun out of orbit.

The World

My mother's kitchen was a sea of blue cupboards
and shiny surfaces, the door was always closed
or just ajar. Sometimes I'd peep in and spot her
dusting packets on shelves, or mopping the floor
smooth as an ice rink. A pot of wilting thyme

sat dying of thirst on the window sill, while outside
a bare hedge ringed our home, fortifying us
from next door. When I asked for water she'd startle
out of her cleaning waltz, spin on the spot, then
take a polished glass from the highest cupboard

and dash to the taps. I'd catch her twisted image
bending in its chrome arm, letting the gush of water
run cold before filling the glass. I'd stand at the door
wanting to break through its icy exterior – the sea
of glass – but knew if I did the world would shatter.

1601

The light of a star that exploded
four hundred years ago
becomes visible to the naked eye.

A prince treads the boards:
This bodes some strange eruption to our state...
The ghost of his father appears, ashen-faced.

Just after four, the second Earl of Essex
is executed for treason. Across the Irish Sea,
men march down to Cork from Donegal.

...Blasts from hell. Crops fail worldwide
due to a volcano in Peru. The Spanish Armada
lies shipwrecked off the Irish coast.

The final stone is placed on the cairn
of Gaelic Rule. Earls take flight for Europe.
Thwarted desire, a bloody end...

Famine sweeps through Russia.
The prince finds himself in a black hole.
There's a special providence in the fall of a sparrow.

Road Signs

What comes back are the birds
that flapped round us:
the weavers' straw nests

hanging from branches like lanterns,
the long-tails sailing past like men
in black ties late for a ball.

In the Drakensberg foothills,
electric-blue bee-eaters
hummed round our rondavel.

The fruit bat that splattered
on our taxi's windscreen, the driver
scooping it up, then spreading

its wings on the dashboard.
A good omen, he told us,
as we flew into deeper darkness.

Anatidaephobia

Anatidaephobia is the fear that somewhere
in the world there is a duck watching you.
No matter where you are, a ringed teal
stares down its long bill searing your skin.
You may be on the lavatory 12,000 feet
above sea level and yet you turn cold
as the leer of a mallard stares up through
the bowl. The trauma often goes back
to a time in childhood when the victim
was scared or injured by a duck.
Perhaps they were flapped at in a park
then tripped and scuffed their knees.
But anatidaephobia can sneak up
on you out of nowhere, it can appear
like the seasonal migration of whooper
swans to the lakes. Anatidaephobia
is irrational, it is a creature with wings
that cuts through everything, it is
the all-seeing eye of a jealous duck.
There is no duck in the sky and yet people
will kill to tell you there is a duck.
While the condition is rare it is possible
that somebody somewhere will develop it now.
There are various evolving suppositions
across a wide spectrum of science
and medicine on anatidaephobia,
many of them appear to be peddled
by quacks. Nevertheless, propounding theories
on quantum mechanics make it even more
probable that there is a duck looking at you.
There is a duck. There is always a duck.
It is a creature with wings that sees
through everything. It is what soaks you
when you wake in the middle of the night.
Some people let it fall off them. Others drown.

Periwinkling

We skirt the edges
of the cove, scouring
crags at low tide,

combing back seaweed hair
braided with beads,
up to our ankles

in rockpool-underworlds.
Dark-marbled clusters,
olive-coloured jumbos

rise to the top.
Blue-black backs plonk
into buckets, squelch between

fingers and thumbs, recoiling
into shells like tiny poems
in their hidden worlds.

We lug a brimming bucket
back home and fill a pan,
watch them toil and bubble.

A sea-tanged steamed-wreathe
breathes its last. I fill a bowl
and, with a pin, open the doors

of their water-world,
picking out slimy whorls
doused in virgin olive oil,

washed down with white wine.
La petite mort marinière.
One little death at a time.

Vacuum

The woman upstairs has been vacuuming
religiously since she came home from hospital,
empty-handed. Scraping a long nozzle across
floorboards, dragging furniture back and forth
against a constant high-pitched thrum,
a delirious humming bird desperate for pollen.
The bag must have enough dirt, hair
and dead skin in it to form another being.

Visiting the Poet

I funnelled down white corridors,
as if through the passages of the mind,
nurses flickering in and out of doors like synapses.
I kept taking wrong turns, reaching dead ends.

Nobody knew his name, even here he was an outsider.
At the end of the left wing I found him
in a warm, airless ward. He was one among the decrepit,
within a clinging smell of stale urine.

Sitting in the far corner, I hardly recognised him,
small in his bleached-blue gown. At first
he didn't know me, but over the slow minutes
something stirred and he uttered my name

pressing it into his lips, gentle as a kiss,
caught it like a dandelion seed on the air
and blew on it... *Adam, Adam*.
Repeating it measuredly like a poem.

It was no flash of inspiration, more
the gradual dawning on a winter's morning,
the watery sun hardly thawing the thick crust of ice.
His drifting eyes, two far-off planets.

I felt like a boy gazing at the night sky
hoping to catch him on his way.
Milk was his new tipple. As I delivered
snippets of news, he sucked little by little

on the nipple of his beaker, eking out the final
nourishments of human kindness. He kept wiping
his nose with a tiny section of tissue, tore off
a wet bit, folded it, then placed it in a plastic bag,

as if he was saving little parchments of life
as it leaked out of him. Though his silver flourish
of hair had a life of its own, his sheet-grey skin
had yielded to gravity... a waning moon

in a distant ellipsis. As I got up to go, he muttered
something under his breath, searching for words
neither of us could find. I left the way I came
along white corridors – out of his mind.

The Flesh and the Spirit

The night before my father died
he looked like a rabid dog
with the shit kicked out of him.

His convexed ribs poked through
the sheets, his sagging torso
a sack of rotten potatoes.

I looked down at the vandalised frame
of his life and stared into the dried-up well
of his eyes, saying his name,

waiting for an echo. I put my ear
to the dusty keyhole of his mouth,
only the shadow of a shallow whisper

stirred in the webbed chamber.
His skin was peeling off
like flakes of plaster.

Half-buried like a child peering out
from the rubble of a war zone.
I took his hand, light as a bird,

and held it in my palm,
kissing the skin that made me.
I licked the flake off my lip

letting it melt on my tongue.
The flesh and the spirit.

Then he spoke to me for the first time.

Poem

(for Ciaran Bermingham)

I found a perfectly polished pebble
the size of a tennis ball washed up
by the morning tide. I took it home
and put it on my table –
a paperweight for words that might
otherwise take wing with the gulls
beyond the window. With time
I noticed it appeared to be growing
until it was too big for the table, so
I placed it by the door as a doorstop.
It kept growing, pushing me aside.
One morning I came downstairs
and noticed a hairline crack running
across it. It started to shake
and a little beak pecked through.

Aisling

Beautiful girl
with a broken harp
who plays on the side
of the street through wind
and rain, her open case catching
coins that flicker as leaves on a lake.
Her plaintive notes which float like pleas
then flee into a whooshing diaspora of rush-
hour traffic as she plinks and plucks more
hay-wire chords that shudder down the
roads and spines of passers-by who do
not know her out-of-tunes have
nothing to do with dexterity
but are due to her harp's
disrepair. Yet she
continues to play
through wind
that blows
her song
away
and rain that collects in her case,
and, because of this, is beautiful.

Apollinaire Smoking

When Apollinaire says to his lover
he wants to smoke at the end of a poem,
he's not talking about cigarettes,
but the thread of fumes hanging momently
above her, reclining in the air,
before withdrawing into the furniture.
He's talking about being spirit,
spirited away, of not being the poet

but the poem, of not disappearing
into nothing or reaching the ends
of the earth. He wants to disperse
into a cloud, a wisp in the wind,
leaving only a trace of himself
on her collar, the post-coital shock
of tousled hair, the tar-breath
still in the mouth.

Fire Bird

I lit a fire and a dove
came swooping

down the chimney
in a burst of flames —

tailspinning
round the room,

bouncing off the furniture,
Jackson Pollocking

the walls in soot.
I opened the window

and it tumbled out,
leaving a whiff

of charred feathers
and a trail of smoke-scrawl.

Verse, Reverse

after Seamus Heaney

The tractor passes to and fro
beyond my window,

cutting lines into the clay,
turning over the dusty

scrub left after last year's harvest,
unfolding clumps of rich humus

which seagulls scatter after
like loose letters

settling on a page. On each turn
the tractor must reverse into position,

the mechanized scythes lower down,
swivelling, before sinking their teeth in,

churning the earth into black
butter, renewing that

which was hidden. An ancient vellum
where the next life is written.

Mythmakers

What I remember now
may not be what happened then.
Nevertheless it remains within,
a croak in my throat.

Like the subject my mother
never could broach.
That year she wouldn't take off
her bottle green cardigan

with the eight-legged silver brooch,
clasped over her left breast.
I dream of spiders nesting
on the insides of walls,

long summer days coming
to a standstill, poking an army
of ants with my grandfather's stick,
as they stream out of a crack

in the curb. My father, somewhere
other, yet keeping abreast.
He rests with me now.
The croak in my throat,

the weight in my chest,
holds fast like an anchor.
Ineluctable. Her cool reproach.
Over and over the eggs hatch.

Would you like me to read you a poem?

after Dennis O'Driscoll

Very well, I thought I'd choose this one. It's a little
long but I think it somewhat explores the avian symbolism
discussed earlier. The first line's non sequitur
never fails to hook readers in. In fact the entire opening
on unrequited love is to die for, so to speak.
There's a bit of an opaque image after that, we won't
go into here, suffice to say the speaker is referring
to his/her mother, and/or sister, perhaps. Lest we forget,
it was after this middle period that the poet relapsed
into brutal silence. The second section is an allusion
to a song aunt Vivienne used to sing, the exact words
of which escape me. But its indefatigable pursuit
of the sublime and meditations on time are unparalleled,
the language being at once astringent and ravishing,
complete like a nucleus, an organism, or orgasm,
you might say. Yet it's the final anti-heroic couplet
that comes across as the most accomplished,
the unshrinking S&M safe word sequence reaches
new dizzying heights. The subtle measure inevitably
comes together and mirrors the matter spawning
a groundswell of vowels that work with and against
the flights of fancy. Perhaps more striking than anything
is its ability to whip off the gauntlet while at the same
time refuse to give itself away entirely, its determination
not to lie down and be buggered to coin a phrase.
Not to mention the bare-cheeked audacity of the dénouement
that lies at its golden centre like a scantily clad
Mediterranean girl turning away, unknowingly exposing
the penumbra of her behind… which in the end is perhaps
its most enduring trait. I should point out some critics
consider its tone naive and whimsical and indicate
that the syncopated rhythm of shifting accents reflects
the theme of arrested development and so on, et cetera.
But I'll leave that for you to determine.
Anyway if you're quite ready I'll begin…

Angry Birds

I'm lost in this world
of crazy kamikazes
selflessly flinging

their harlequin bodies
against timber planks,
panes of glass and metal bars

to snuff out a spread of swine.
Wasted with flu,
the only thing I can do

is play a game on my phone,
the single premise of which
is to catapult birds

against a litter of pigs
hidden in various structures.
Struck down with a fever

over a hundred, health
feels like a childhood
that can't be recaptured.

Poorly, as the prodigal son
who squandered everything.
I can create chaos

with the stroke of my finger,
send raptors to collapse
complex constructions,

pickaxing and squawking
into scaffolding. Shot starlings
explode into formations,

tumbling down on a battalion
of pug-nose snorters
who keep growing and dying

with every level of delirium.
I can only dream
that these feathered-friends

hold some answer —
that they are my deliverers
carrying me home.

Wherever that may be.

Operation: Cleansing the Leaven

'The desperate plight of the Palestinian people,
the central factor of world unrest.'
                                    Harold Pinter

Observers
spend the weeks
in a flurry

of housecleaning
to expunge
every scrap

from all parts
of the home.
Flour is treated

as vermin
and must be quashed
at all costs.

Law requires
the elimination
of olive-sized,

or larger, quantities
of leavening.
But a good housekeeper

leaves no seed
unturned, the cracks
of kitchen counters

are thoroughly scrubbed
to remove any traces,
however small.

Then, when every last molecule
has been disposed of,
observers wash their hands

and every part of their person,
to avoid any suggestion
of contamination.

Rag and Bone Man

'Never send to know for whom the bells tolls; it tolls for thee.

John Donne

All day the sea's been in my head,
frothing and jostling over the jetty
heaving in great swells, white lines
edging the coast, sparking like nerve-
endings from the cliff's fingers –
licks of wave-quiffs spraying back.

Come evening as the tide recedes,
the storm dies as quickly as it came.
The sky clears and the sun dissolves
in a white-washed haze. The sea
changes face, a grey sheen of polished
metal or wrought iron, flat as slate.

I go out with my bucket, clambering
down among the rocks and crags;
two cormorants flail and scatter
like bin bags. Hundreds of shells cluttered
like broken crockery around my feet:
clams, cockles, muscles, all prised open

and jettisoned by the curlews and gulls.
I root among the hollow shells, peel back
the wet hair of weeds where a few hidden
periwinkles cling. I must look like an awful
god, beachcombing for surviving scraps.
A giant rag and bone man.

Tomas Transformer

The one-handed pianist
strolls over the frozen lake

and climbs a snowy hill
to the other side.

Toy-size, he stands beside
a single silver birch.

Light breaks the clouds,
a sword slicing across snow.

Scarecrow and maiden,
bride and groom join hands.

Rathgar Rose

Our slow-budding bloom is black
as night, or at least bruise-purple
like summer twilights in Terenure.

A tight blackberry knot
of sugar paper petals waiting to happen.
It opens eventually, then suddenly

offering up its potent perfume
to all who pass these sleepy avenues
of red-bricked Edwardian villas —

a crow's throw from where
Sunny Jim was born.
A few restless nights

before they fall on the lawn.
Leaving only deadheads,
blushing thoughts.

Foxglove Fantasia

I turned off the usual track and found an entrance
to where pines had been felled a few years back.
Now it was all green with life, but more fantastically
it was teeming with foxgloves as tall as I – bulging
purple bells. I walked up the hill to get the full impact
of the vista and stood in the middle of the haze.
I put my head inside their peeling petals. It brought
me back to Barcelona, climbing Sagrada Família,
peeping out onto surreal spires: the hum of bees
playing the keys of clarinets, stacks of candy floss,
wispy wizard hats, swollen grapes on the vine,
chocolate fountains oozing down honeycomb towers,
coquettish cotton dresses opening in the breeze,
whispering to the birds and the bees: *Look at me,*
look at me! The world is whatever you want it to be.

Rough Metaphors

(after Rumi)

I've come to the edge of myself.
There's no way out.
I've reached the final junction.

The signposts are mirrors
that reflect back the way I came.
These are rough metaphors.

I could polish and shape them
until they are round
and smooth as crystal balls.

I could tear my eyes
out of my skull and replace them
with these other marvels.

Solstice Drive

Fans whir, the engine purrs. The stereo glares
blue and red. A green glow flashes 07:00.

Frozen vapour hazes the windscreen, stars
sparkle overhead. Otherwise all is darkness.

Fullbeams stun ghost-trails of fog,
the coiled lane loosens like lace.

A world comes slowly back to itself
like an old idea. The heavens turn

as the car steers. Nebulous fields
are released from invisible chains.

Rows of houses beetle past on a carousel.
An electric flatline quivers on the horizon

then fades, as if my turning has reversed time.
On the bridge, a jurassic bird unravels

its undying burden…
a black flag flapping at halfmast.

*

I turn into the station, bleep the car to sleep.
A brisk wind cuts across the platform.

Trains tremble between synchronized clocks.
I step into a steel husk, a miasma of metal and glass.

We push out into a tunnel, memory is jogged
by a familiar pull. The body shocks

with the shudder of engines towards light.
Then, we screech to a stop like a breached birth.

We start-stop, then begin again and are rolling.
Fields, towns, woods I know, play-back under me,

a filmreel snaking to life. Everything glossed
in the silver sheen of night's afterbirth.

Unreal earth I am betrothed to, becoming
luminous, I feel it in my bones,

a knife driving through frosted hedgerows.
Across the miles of open planes

it starts to crown, laser-beaming between
my eyes. A laser beam that is my life.

The Great Book of Ireland

A great book never ends, but returns to the start.
This Heisenberg principle, this archaeological art
whose only certainty is entropy. This book
of babel, a whorl of words. From, 'Clapton is God'
to Beckett's last scrawls scored on his deathbed
on the death of his father, before casting his pen
aside – like Excalibur – to put out the light.
The stray work of Sweeney and O'Grady
that may one day be unearthed by a scholar,
hidden in another's lines, or obscured in chiaroscuro.
A war of words mushrooms, jostles for elbow room.
Words wedged edgeways along the pages' borders.
This vellum script, this elm case, felled from a tree
planted by Yeats, shakes hands with the scribes
whose scripts shone a light from the dark edge
of Europe. This million euro body of words
we hold so dear is never as dear until it lives
in our minds; ringed round the gyres of time.
May we keep you close, a page always open.
We pray for your longevity and legacy in this age
of all ages where we rage against a storm
of bureaucracy. We'll preserve you in the perfect
temperature, under protective glass. The jealous
artefact of our fractured lives, bound together.
Unfetter these words, unlock the scores,
their cyphers. May they live again in our mouths.
To read is to go back over the tracks;
lest we forget our dark fathers.
This blessed blot, this calf, this turf, this Ireland.

(Commissoned to celebrate University College Cork's acquisition of *The Great Book of Ireland*, 2014.)

Home

The house is dark and quiet.
I go into my room
and the other rooms begin to stir.

I hear the opening and closing of doors,
buzz of immersion,
water-trickles from the shower.

Kitchen drawers slide open,
the dishwasher empties its insides,
cutlery clatters, pots and pans are put in their place.

Coffee percolates through the rooms,
seeps into floorboards, sifts between woodlice
and mice nesting in the insulation.

Voices murmur, their bass note chorus
creates an echo chamber.
Toilets are flushed, teeth brushed.

Stairs creak under the dull thud of feet,
loosening knots down the spine.
The front door opens, sucking in

a gasp of air, then slams shut.
The house falls silent.
I sink deeper into the foundations,

the roots of the garden.
An underground river moves below
that leads to a bottomless sea.

The Talking Tree Alphabet

'I know death hath ten thousand several doors
For men to take their exits; and 'tis found
They go on such strange geometrical hinges,
You may open them both ways: any way, for heaven-sake,
So I were out of your whispering.'

from *The Duchess of Malfi*, John Webster

Elm

The elm is full of noise tonight,
flapping its leafy branches
like a majestic bird pushing up
against the underworld.

Rowan

For her heart, the princess asked Finbar
to fetch a branch of rowan berries
blooming on the other side of the river
guarded by the one-eyed ogre.
Her devoted lover swam across
to the forbidden enclosure
where berries blinked ruby necklaces –
small dancing flames on black-tipped wicks.
The ogre came thumping towards him,
wielding a knuckled cudgel, took one swing,
thwacking the air, missed and toppled
down with a whump on his back.
Finbar, never taking his eye off the prize,
climbed on the ogre's belly
and bounced and jounced and plucked
the thickest branch of finest berries
and brought them back to his princess.
He fed her the bitter-sweet intoxicating seeds
then, ringed within the blushing beads,
they made love on the forest floor.
Her feet took root in the earth,
inside her belly grew a tree of fire,
her arms gnarled and knotted
into branches, her hair flamed red
and she vanished within the dark bark.
Finbar went to fetch an axe
to try to cut his princess out,
but when he returned a dozen
other rowans had grown
and he wasn't sure which
switch of the woods she was...
The earth shook beneath him,
a vast shadow swallowed the sun.

Pear

In the orchard the son
asked his father where
everything in the world
came from. The father
plucked a pear from
a branch, broke its flesh
in half and gave his son
a seed, then asked him
to crack it open and tell
him what he saw inside.
The son bit into its husk
and said there was nothing
there. They continued
through the orchard without
a word between them.

Birch

Everyone has a picture of that iconic dress
in their head, the silver one that ballooned

and swirled above her legs on the subway grate.
But few know the story of when she first tried it on

saying she wanted to become
as the silver birch she sat under as a child –

the one that lit up like a maypole after rain
and had the sweet tang of bourbon.

Whenever she was lost she'd close her eyes and listen
to its whispers as it succumbed to the breeze.

Now she had become the dream, yet behind
her blithe smile was the studied model

directed to fight the updraught, just enough to show
trembling legs, but not to reveal anything else.

Ash

Leaf sounds sing like a children's choir,
the sun splashes the tips of their tongues.
Boughs and branches rise and twist,
the arms of whirling dervishes.
Each note gives a flash of the mirror within.
Everything grows upwards like the child
reaching towards his father.

Oak

The old oak is our father
coming home late at night,
turning his key in the door,
leaving it off the latch.

The leaves are still falling.
I hear his slippered footsteps
shuffle on the stairs, scuff
along boards. He stifles

a cough opening my door
and releases the catch
from the window, taking
my breath as the curtains

mushroom. A pattern
of webbed branches frames
the moon. His great shadow
bows low and creaks

down the years, pressing his
whiskered cheeks to my brow,
whispering *good night*.
The old oak swishes and moans,

low mutterings meander
through the house. The wind
brushes my face, the sound
of leaves patting the pane.

The moon is in the wind
and the wind is in the bough
and the bough is in the door
that our father leaves open.

Blackthorn

tear across the valley,
criss-crossing fields
like a madman's scrawl.

A malady of inflictions.
Each one twisted
and crooked like a crone.

Earth-mother turned sour
after years of minus temperatures
and indomitable squalls.

More scrub than tree,
yet she still shows glimmers
of her maiden fair,

when sloe-berries burden
cracked knuckles
and white flowers shroud

her demented crown.
Come once more my ravaged whore
and let us kiss at the point of death.

Fir

(for Paulo)

That spring, my brother and I discovered
the alleys behind the housing estate
on the edge of town. After an hour
of tunnelling along paths that tapered

into country tracks the landscape opened
on a sweep of firs that spread out
on the other side of the valley.
Each green shade was a mosaic scale,

a dragon's tail trailing off into the horizon.
We ran down the hill till we were outside
its verdant border and stepped into
the picture. There was no entrance,

just rows of furry claws brushing together.
Cross-hatched branches snagged our clothes,
a lethargic weight hung like smoke.
The ground was a rotting compost,

clusters of stumps poked out
like desecrated graves. The creak and sigh
of a lame fir lurched forward like a witch.
It was as if we'd stumbled upon a cemetery

that had lain hidden for centuries.
We wandered in circles not knowing
which way we'd entered, as though
we were treading inside the earth.

Chestnut

(for Mike)

I came down to the bottom of the stairs
and found him sitting there in his chair
reading the paper. He looked up and smiled
and said it's been a long time. I said,
how can this be, you're dead? He admitted
that was true, he couldn't explain that.
I started to cry and he stood up and wiped
my tears. Then I must be dead. Don't be
silly, he whispered. Where have you been?
I don't really know… It was like I was lost
in the cupboard under the stairs or inside
the hollow of the chestnut at the bottom
of the garden. The funny thing was I didn't
feel particularly lost. I wasn't sure if you
were home or not but I saw the light on.
I hope you don't mind, I fixed myself a drink?
It's been a long time, can you forgive me?
I want to tell you everything. I walked
to the window listening to his voice tail off,
the leaves waving like hands.

Willow

I head to the park
and sit on a bench
under a shower of willows.

No one is around
save for a couple cooing
in the gloom.

I open the book
I've been dying to finish
and I'm taken

into another world
of freezing landscapes.
The willows shiver above,

brushing my shoulder.
I look up from the page,
the lovers have gone.

I return to the book,
but there are no words.
Perhaps I only imagined them.

Elder

A low sun hovers over
the roofs like a third eye
lasering through a maze
of black branches.

An old man sits on a bench
behind bars
of shadowed trunks.
One by one the leaves let go,

a head of wild copper
carpets the ground.
A small girl passing
tells her mother the leaves

are magic, she's never noticed
autumn before. She scoops
them off the ground – giant
coins in her tiny hands –

then shells them out
to her mother, one after
the other. The sun moves
behind the elder.

Spindle

The night is an animal
shaped out of time.
We try to stroke it,
it's not there.

We look it in the eye,
it turns into a spindle.
The all-seeing pink berries

peel back and shine,
till dawn sparrows
peck them,
and all our lights go out.

Aspen

Silver strands startle the night,
towers of babel lick the air,
hundreds of tongues purl.
The city hums with a surge

of language. I pick a leaf and place it
on my tongue. Under ground,
a single voice purrs through a network
of tunnels that leads out

of language. At the centre is a door
that does not open
but can be entered
when the right word is spoken.

Gorse

This morning rows of yellow flowers
flash along the bank, waving their petals
like a throng of eager faces. I open
the window and breathe them in.

Perhaps I should say something, address
them like a king, or a rock star on stage
asking the lights to be turned towards
the crowd before breaking into 'Pablo Honey'?

But they are the constellations, the supernovas
being born and dying at the same time.
I could go outside, pluck one by the throat,

though I know beneath that gold are thorns
that draw blood and score the heart completely.

Pine

(for Paula)

We drove through dusk
up the mountain pass,
pushing through villages
without stopping.
The promise of a last

petrol station never arrived.
The gauge flashed red.
The clutch kept slipping.
Darkness fell,
rubbing its thick musk

against the windscreen,
dragging its black tail over us.
The husks of old tyres
piled high like totems
on the side of the road

seemed to mark the end
of a civilization. We were
ascending towards the next
century, the dust from
the lowlands scattered behind us.

The car started to steam
and chug like a sick animal.
None of us spoke, willing
ourselves forward; our heads
getting lighter, the air

turning sweeter with pine.
When we reached the peak
I put her into neutral and we
rolled with the windows
down, the sound of tyres

tearing over tarmac,
the wind whistling in our ears.
Then, out of the blackness
a cluster of lights appeared
as if the heavens were below us.

The Hedge

'There is somewhere in our lives a great unsolved love.'
from *Madrigal*, Tomas Tranströmer

HE

The hedge is just high enough that when people pass all I can see is the top of their heads. I cannot resist looking away from my monitor to see people's bodies disappear, leaving only a disembodied head to slide over manicured foliage. If I stand up and look out the corner of the window I can see body and head reunited past the end of the hedge. But as I sit at my desk where I am now it's the perfect position to watch floating heads. Naturally, the heads themselves have no idea that at the minute of passing my window they are being dismembered. They simply drift past like aloof balloons.

SHE

I expect you've gone on one of your jaunts. Did you take your binoculars? You always like to get up close to things. I remember when you first saw me you couldn't get close enough. I grew in front of you, until I was out of focus and swiped the binoculars from your face. It was my neck you commented on. Do you remember what I said? I yapped I'm not an animal in a zoo! You concurred and tripped over a stone because you had lost perspective without your binoculars.

HE

Since my arrival, I have been walking in woodland just beyond the house. Wildflowers and grasses carpet the ground. The trees themselves are mostly trembling aspen. A dazzling kaleidoscope of colours: blue, purple, red, orange and yellow. I walk in the woods at least once a day. I watch the leaves and branches sway in the wind and I begin to sway with them. It is a little dance we share. They look out at me suggestively, perched on their branches. The leaves stay, they do not blow away.

SHE
A man came by the house today. He said he was looking for you. He was carrying a briefcase. I said you were not home. He asked when you'd be back. I asked who was enquiring. He thought it would be better if he talked to you. He didn't say another word but handed me a card. Are you in some kind of trouble?

HE
As I got up to draw the curtains last night, there was another head bobbing up as the streetlights were being turned on. Only this head was not the usual bouncing, floating balloon that passes, it was something else. It had hair all over its face and a long turned-up nose and pointed ears. A fox. It slid by about seven a.m. Floating freely over the top of the hedge. But this floating head did not reach the end of the hedge. Halfway along, the floating head stopped and started to grow smaller. Then it disappeared behind a door in the house opposite. It turns out that the new people, who moved in at No. 6, are a family of foxes.

SHE
Perhaps I was too hasty to the man at the door and should assist him in his inquiry. At least then there'd be two of us working together for your whereabouts. I think I'll give him a ring. I can tell him the story of how we met and see what evidence he might glean. I have no doubt he's a detective. He has the nose of a good P.I. Maybe I'll come up smelling of roses yet, which is a damn sight better than eating daisies.

HE
The foxes' heads have become more frequent. I stay in all day by the fire, reading the same damn paper. It seems everyone is at each other's throats. But I cannot get these foxes out of my head. I'm biding my time. I'm writing a strong letter to the landlord. I have noticed of late there is water getting in from the ceiling, dripping into my room.

Not only that, but ivy is breaking and entering through the cracks around the window. I have told the landlord that while I am composing my letter this house is decomposing. I have said that when I live in a house I mean that house to be a house, solid and airtight. I do not want to live in a tree house. If I wanted to live in a tree house, I would have chosen to live in the woods, but I told him I have stopped going to the woods since the woods are coming to me.

SHE

The man at the door didn't just leave me his card. He left me something else; he slipped it under the door. I assume it's for you. I'm sitting here in the dark with it.

HE

The foxes are entertaining this evening. They have not invited me. The room is full of chatter, music, laughter and something that resembles a parlour game. In the gloom, I can make out a woman trapped in the middle of all this. She is dancing for a fox. Any moment one of them is going to snap. I could intervene and smash an ornament, or slip in when no one is looking. I decide to take a closer look and creep across the road.

SHE

There was a precious titbit I omitted in the story of our meeting. When I took your binoculars from you, I lifted them up to my eyes and you were tiny, like a tadpole swimming in a Petri dish, or a god in a cloud. How peculiar you looked, a grown man the size of a pea standing in front of me. Small and distant down the end of a tunnel. That's what falling in love is, you said, like seeing God through the wrong end of binoculars. Are you suggesting you are God, I asked?

HE

The largest fox wears a torn vest and keeps scratching his crotch, licking his lips as he watches the dancing girl. I see a gap in the window and climb in. Nobody notices me at first, but soon the fox in the torn vest catches sight of me and grits his teeth. He walks up to me and presses his head against mine as if I were a pair of binoculars. We are eye to eye. The girl scurries to the door. The keys are in the fox's eyes. He orders me to sit down and thrusts a beer in my hand. Suddenly the girl falls into my lap, laughing hysterically. I push her off and she starts yelling, banging my chest and pulling at my vest. I grab her hand and we run for the door that opens out onto a back street I'd not noticed before. She pulls me towards her and shoves her tongue down my throat. As she pulls away, she takes a key out of her mouth.

SHE

The last look of love we had you took my breath away. Your hands so close, I still feel their warm grip. As soon as you let go I felt your absence. You are both a comfort and a thief. But my powers of speech and cognitive faculties remain intact. The problem is my body. I can't see my body. Is it still visible through your binoculars, I wonder?

HE

Last night I dreamt I was my father asleep dreaming of his father. In the dreams my grandfather was also asleep dreaming he was his father in a wood. The soft breeze on his face, the sounds of the water, the tang of the trembling aspen. The path trails off and I see five foxes are trotting beside me. They don't seem half as strange in the woods. Then I see a beautiful head growing out of a bough, spreading its branches in all directions.

Notes on Poems

1601 – The italics in this poem are from *Hamlet*. 1601 is believed to be the year the play was first performed. It is also the year of the battle of Kinsale, which brought an end to Gaelic rule in Ireland during the Elizabethan conquest.

ANGRY BIRDS – The last line in this poem is a quote from the last line of Elizabeth Bishop's poem 'Questions of Travel'.

OPERATION: CLEANSING THE LEAVEN – Cleansing the Leaven refers to the Jewish religious practice of eliminating all traces of bread or flour from people's homes on the eve of the Passover. Operation: Cleansing the Leaven is the name given for the 1948 campaign which saw one million Palestinians killed or displaced.

TOMAS TRANSFORMER is written after Swedish poet Tomas Tranströmer (1931-2015)

RATHGAR ROSE – 'Sunny Jim' was James Joyce's pet name as a child. Joyce was born in the Dublin suburb of Rathgar.

THE GREAT BOOK OF IRELAND – was commissoned to celebrate University College Cork's acquisition of *The Great Book of Ireland*, 2014. It is a huge vellum book, which includes the work of hundreds of Ireland's writers and artists.

GORSE – *Pablo Honey* is the title of Radiohead's first LP, released 1993.

ADAM WYETH lives in Dublin. His critically acclaimed collection, *Silent Music*, was Highly Commended by the Forward Poetry Prize. His poetry has won and been commended in many international competitions, including The Bridport Poetry Prize, The Arvon Poetry Prize and The Ballymaloe Poetry Prize. His work appears in several anthologies including *The Forward Prize Anthology* (2012 Faber), *The Best of Irish Poetry* (Southword 2010) and *The Arvon 25th Anniversary Anthology*. In 2016, he was selected as a *Poetry Ireland Review* Rising Generation poet. Adam's second book *The Hidden World of Poetry: Unravelling Celtic Mythology in Contemporary Irish Poetry* was published by Salmon in 2013. The book contains poems from Ireland's leading poets followed by sharp essays that unpack each poem and explore its Celtic mythological references. Adam has also had several plays produced in Ireland and Germany including *Hang Up*, produced by Broken Crow (2013), which was adapted into a film in 2014 and premiered at Cork's International Film Festival. It was also staged in 2015 in Berlin as part of 'An Evening of Adam Wyeth' at Theaterforum Kreuzberg. Adam runs online Creative Writing workshops and editing programmes at adamwyeth.com and Fishpublishing.com.